THIS BOOK
BELONGS TO

____

____

____

Vicky Rasinske

No protion of this book may be reproduced in whole or in part shared with others, stored in a retriveal system,digitized or transmitted in any from without written persission from the author.

COLOR TEST

Basic tips of Drawing!

★ A little bit of art theory is always good to know, Lets start........

★ All you need is a pencil,eraser and a piece off paper!

★ Draw lightly at first because you might need to erase some lines as you work.

★ Add details according to the diagrams but dont worry about being perfect. Artists frequently make mistakes they just find ways to make their mistakes look interesting.

★ Dont worry if your drawing dont turn out the way you want them to , just keep practicing ! Sometimes drawing the same thing just a few times will help.

★ Once you have finished your drawing in pencil you can trace it with a black fineliner pen and color or paint it to your liking.

Turn the page for some cool composition ideas!!!

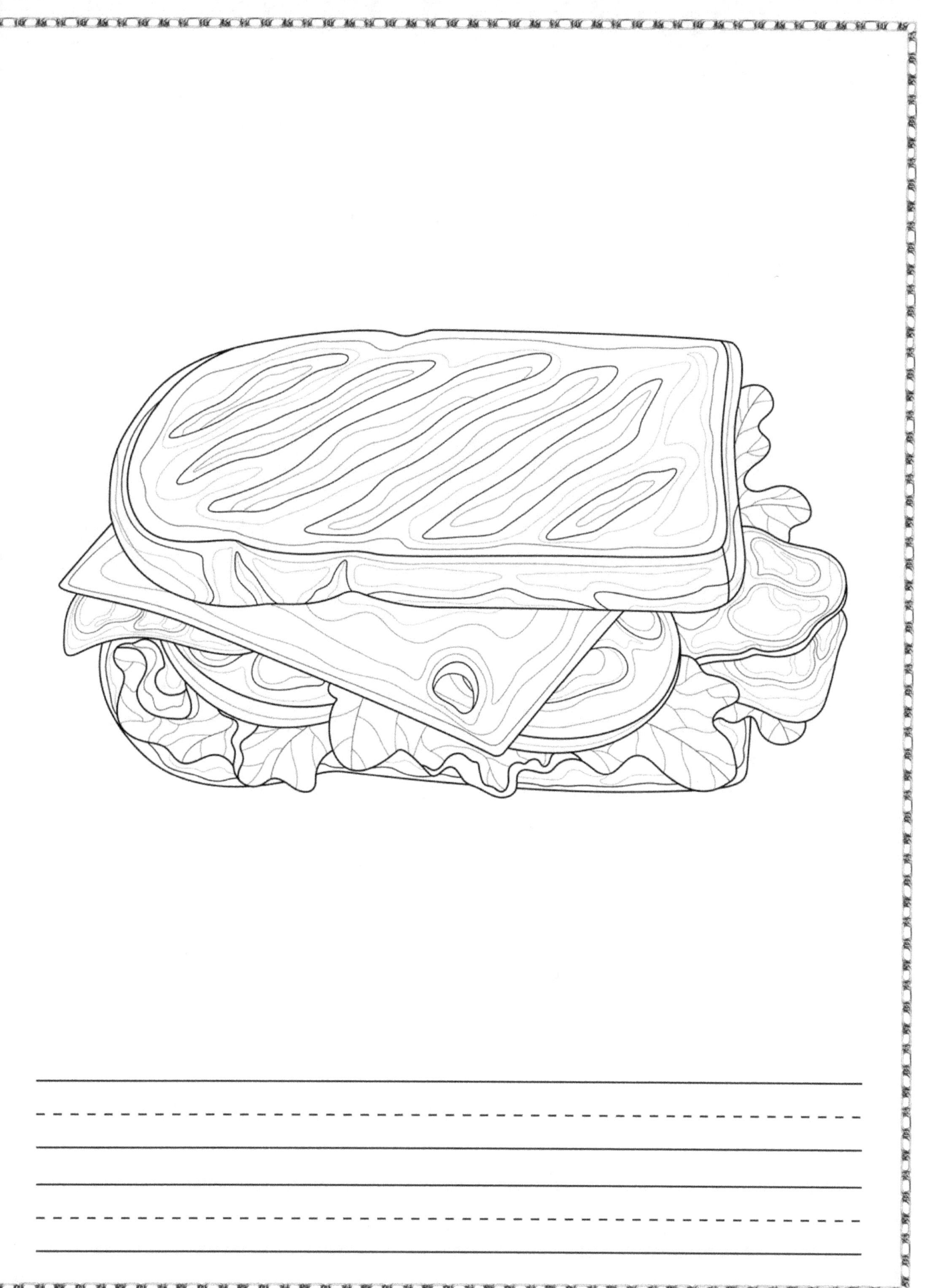

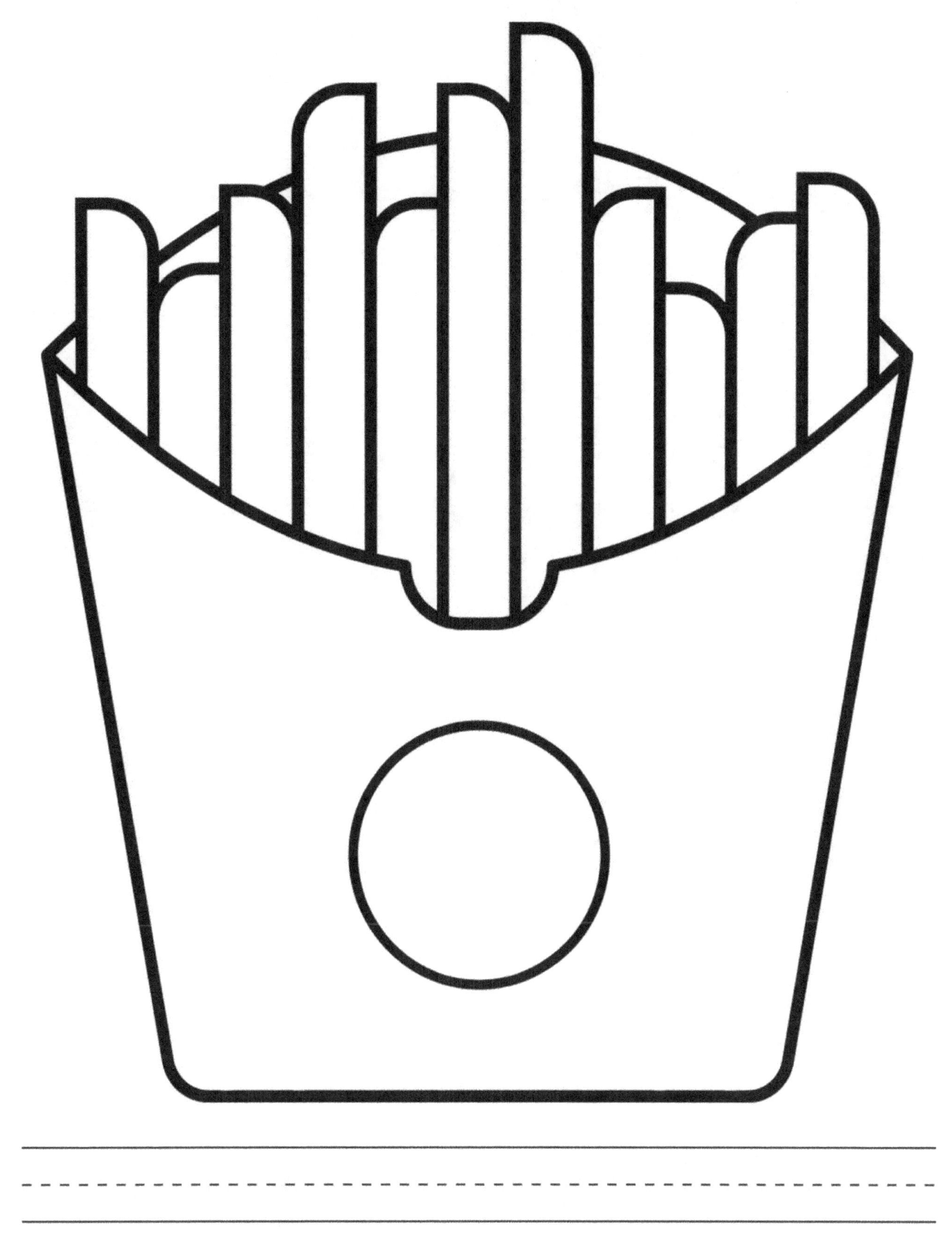

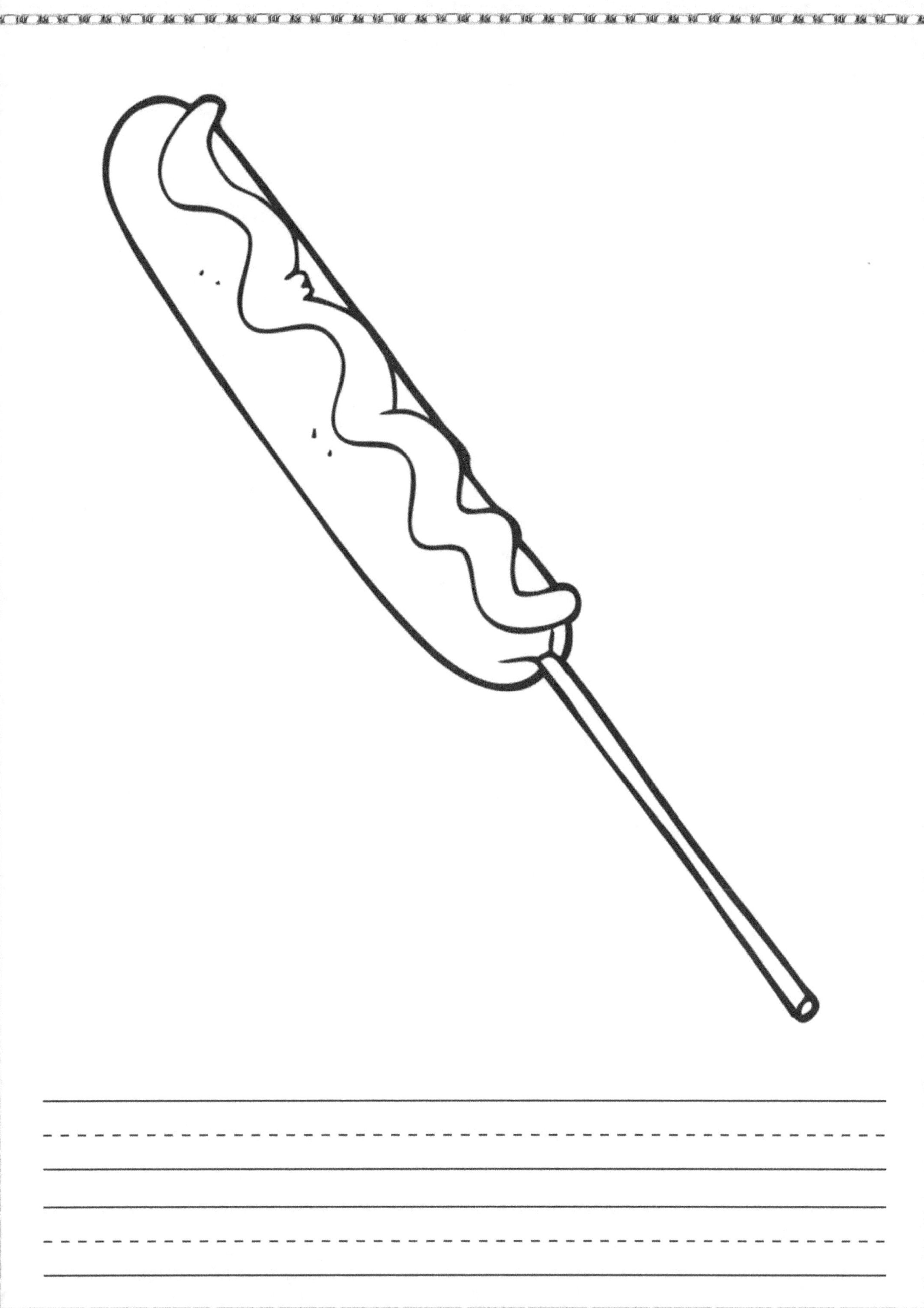

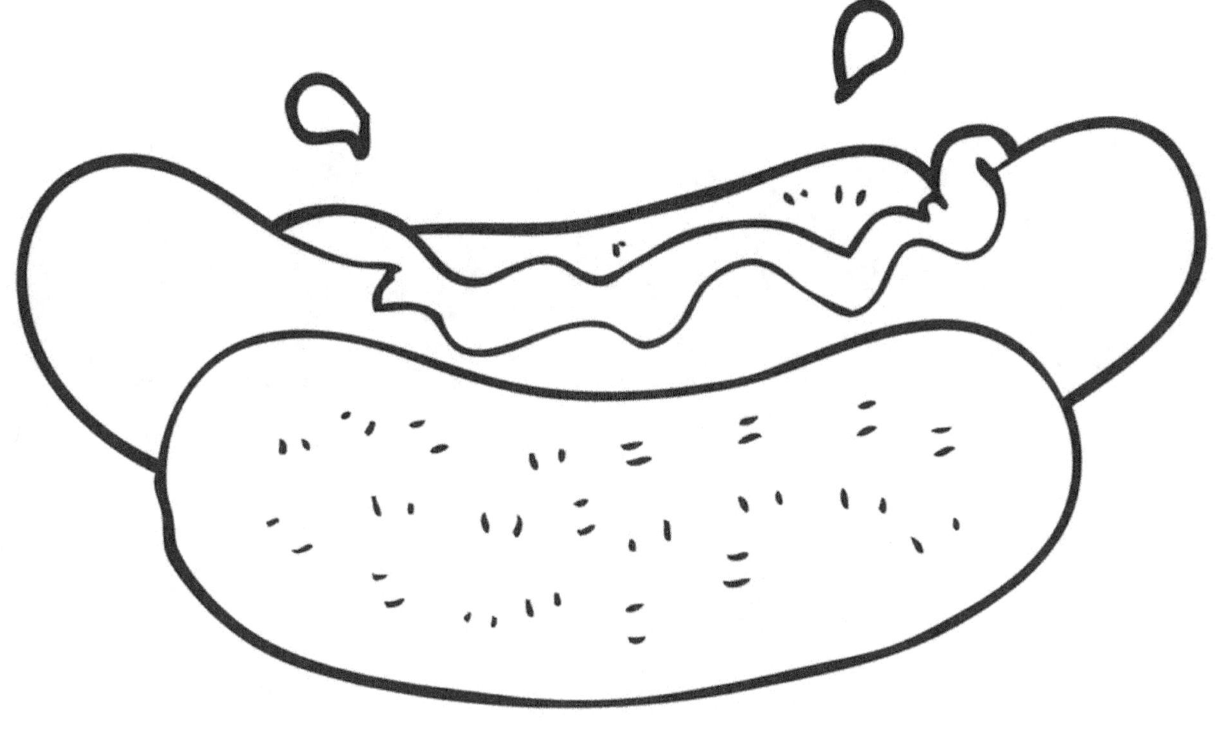

HOT~DOG

PIZZA

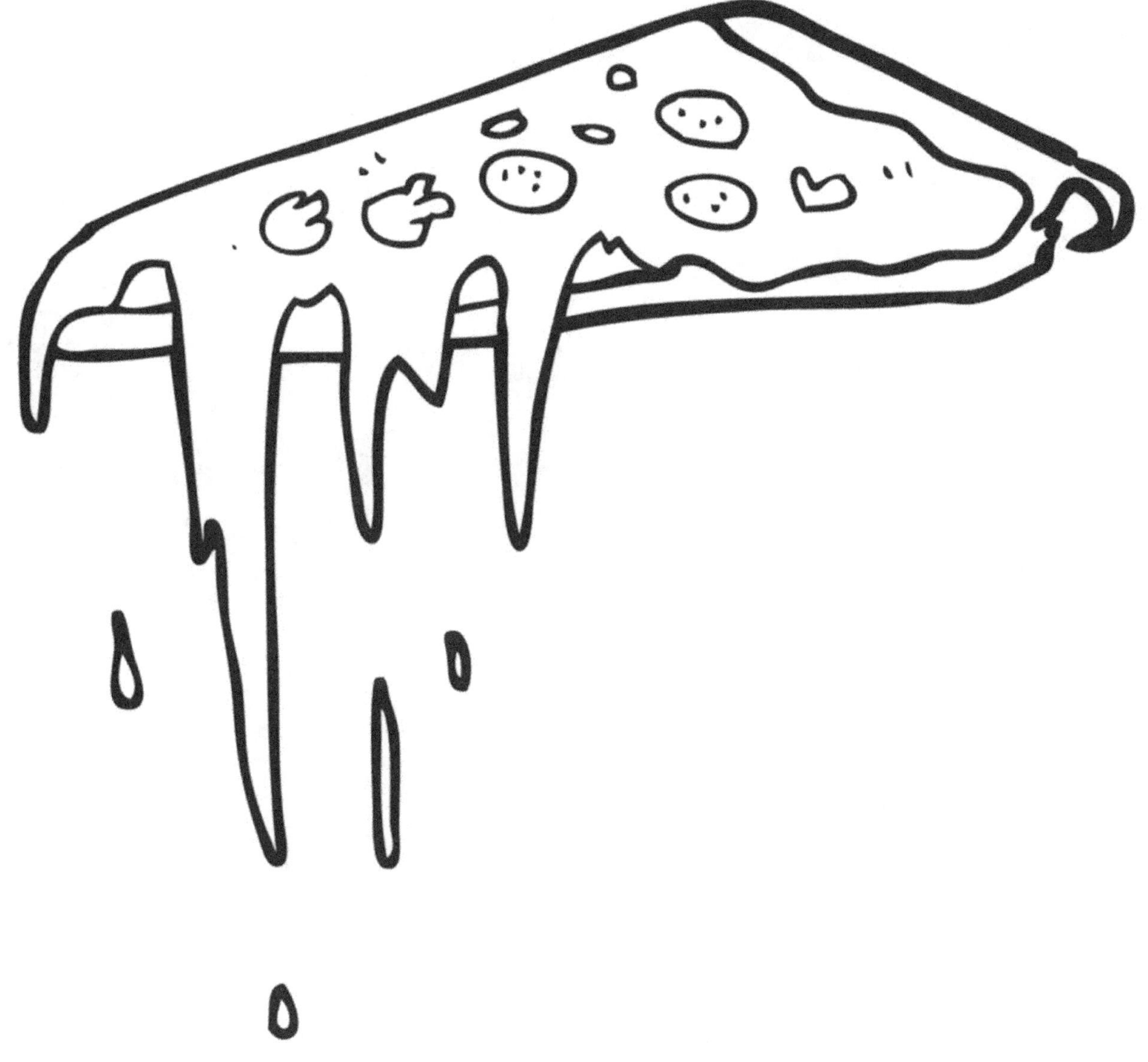

Please consider writing a review!

THANK
YOU

www.ingramcontent.com/pod-product-compliance
Lightning Source LLC
Chambersburg PA
CBHW081955260726
48658CB00010BB/2624